SCRIPTURE COLORING BOOK

those who know
your name trust
in you, for you,
Lord, have never
forsaken those
who seek you.

Psalm 9:10

PSALM 25
LEAD ME IN
YOUR TRUTH
ALL THE PATHS
OF THE LORD ARE STEADFAST
LOVE.
TEACH ME YOUR PATHS.

We love because He first loved us.
John 4:19

PSALM 116
I WILL CALL ON THE NAME of the LORD
CUP of SALVATION
WHAT SHALL I RETURN TO THE LORD?

I and My Father are one.
John 10:30

PSALM 107
Let them thank the Lord for the Lord's
Steadfast Love
Let them tell of the Lord's deeds...
The Lord saved them.
Some were sick.
They cried to the Lord in their trouble.
The Lord's steadfast love endures forever.

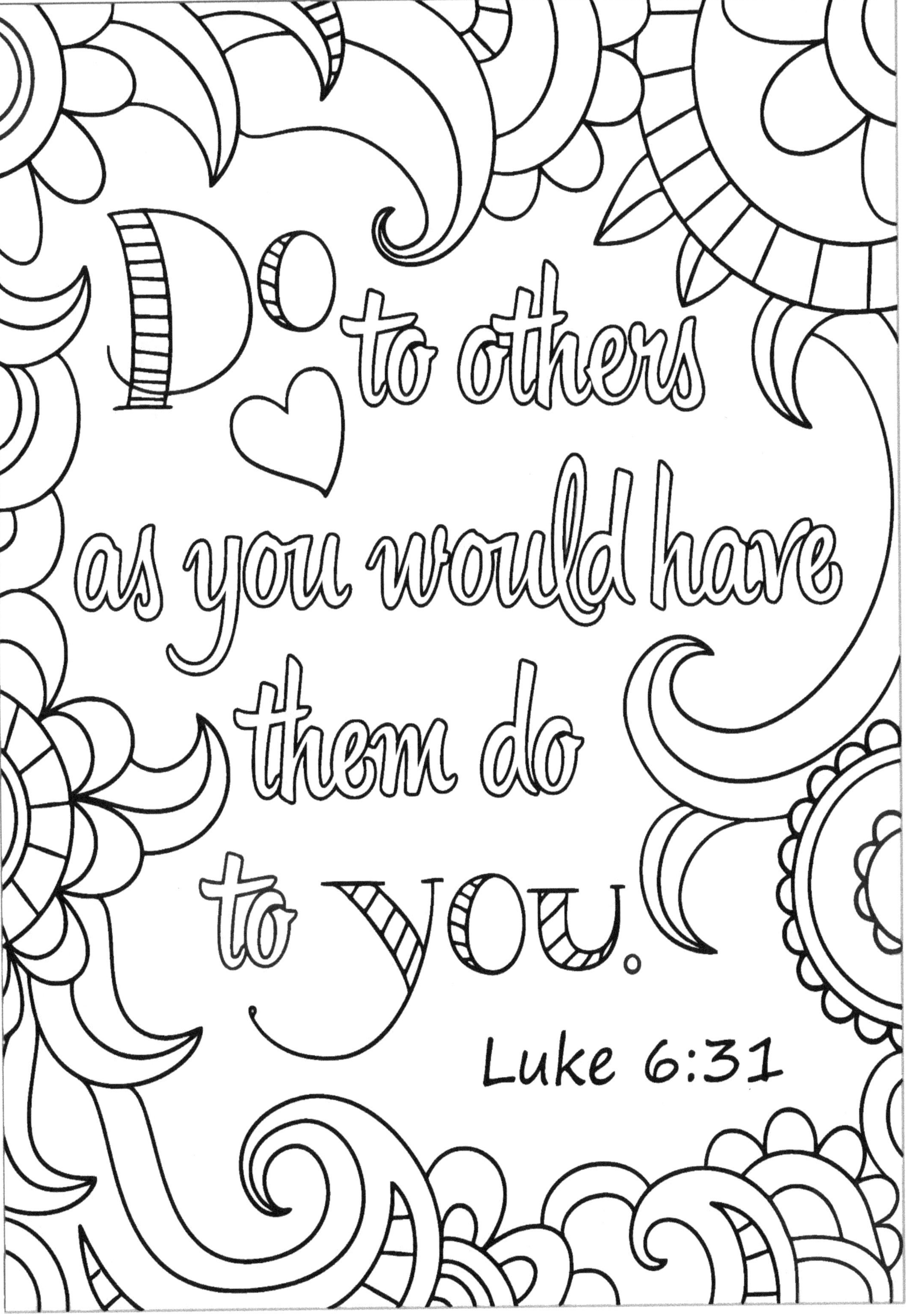
Do to others
as you would have
them do
to you.
Luke 6:31

BE GRACIOUS TO ME, O LORD, FOR I AM IN DISTRESS.

Be joyful
in hope,
patient in
affliction,
faithful
in prayer.
Romans 12:12

PSALM 31
YOU ARE MY GOD. MY TIMES ARE IN YOUR HAND.
BE GRACIOUS TO ME, O LORD, FOR I AM IN DISTRESS.

The LORD
is my rock, my fortress and my deliverer;
MY GOD IS MY ROCK,
in whom I take refuge, my shield and the horn of my salvation,
MY STRONGHOLD.
PSALM 18:2

PSALM 22
ALL THE ENDS OF THE EARTH SHALL TURN TO THE LORD.
THOSE WHO SEEK THE LORD SHALL PRAISE THE LORD.
THE LORD HEARD WHEN I CRIED TO THE LORD.

May he give you
the desires of your
HEART
and make all your plans
succeed
Psalm 20:4

One thing I ask from the Lord, this only do I seek:
that I may dwell in the house of the Lord
all the days of my life,
to gaze on the beauty of the Lord
and to seek him in his temple.
Psalm 27:4

Lord
MY
GOD
I called to you for help,
and you healed me.
Psalm 30:2

But I will
Sing
of your strength, in the morning
I will sing of your love, for you
are my fortress, my refuge
in times of trouble
Psalm 59:16

create in me a
pure heart
O God
and renew a
steadfast spirit
within me
Psalm 51:10

You are the most excellent of men
and your lips have been
anointed with grace,
since God has blessed you
forever
You are the most
excellent of men
Psalm 45:2

I DESIRE TO DO YOUR WILL,
MY GOD;
YOUR LAW IS WITHIN
MY HEART.
PSALM 40:8

THE LORD IS MY
STRENGTH AND
MY SHIELD;
MY HEART TRUSTS IN HIM,
AND HE HELPS ME.
MY HEART
LEAPS FOR JOY,
AND WITH MY SONG
I PRAISE HIM.
PSALM 28:7

I will instruct you
and teach you in the
way you should go;
I will counsel you
with my
loving eye on you.
Psalm 32:8

I PRAISE YOU BECAUSE I AM FEARFULLY AND WONDERFULLY MADE; YOUR WORKS ARE WONDERFUL, I KNOW THAT FULL WELL
Psalm 139:14

The fear of the Lord is the beginning of
WISDOM;
all who follow his precepts have
good understanding.
To him belongs eternal praise.
Psalm 111:10

SEARCH ME, GOD,
and know my heart; test me and know my anxious thoughts
Psalm 139:23

Taste and see
that the
Lord is good;
blessed is the one who takes refuge in him.
Psalm 34:8

Cast your cares on the Lord
and he will sustain you;
he will never let the
righteous be shaken.
Psalm 55:22

I LIE DOWN AND SLEEP
I WAKE AGAIN BECAUSE THE LORD
SUSTAINS ME
Psalm 3:5

LEAD ME,
LORD
IN YOUR RIGHTEOUSNESS
BECAUSE OF MY ENEMIES
MAKE YOUR WAY STRAIGHT
BEFORE ME.
Psalm 5:8

The Lord has dealt with me
according to my righteousness;
according to the
cleanness of my hands
he has rewarded me.
Psalm 18:20

THE SALVATION
of the righteous comes from the Lord;
he is their stronghold
IN TIME OF TROUBLE.
Psalm 37:39

BUT LET ALL WHO TAKE REFUGE IN YOU BE GLAD;
LET THEM EVER SING FOR JOY.
SPREAD YOUR PROTECTION OVER THEM,
THAT THOSE WHO LOVE YOUR
NAME MAY REJOICE IN YOU.

Psalm 5:11

MY SHIELD IS GOD MOST HIGH,
WHO SAVES
THE UPRIGHT IN HEART.
PSALM 7:10

It is God who arms me with strength and keeps my way secure.
Psalm 18:32

Hear my cry for help,
my King and
my God,
for to you I pray.
Psalm 5:2

THE UNFOLDING
OF YOUR WORDS
GIVES LIGHT;
IT GIVES
UNDERSTANDING
TO THE SIMPLE.
PSALM 119:130

GIVE
THANKS
TO THE LORD,
FOR HE IS GOOD;
HIS LOVE
ENDURES FOREVER.
PSALM 118:1

Open my eyes
that I may see
wonderful things
in your law.
Psalm 119:18

He heals the brokenhearted
and binds up their wounds.
Psalm 147:3

THE LORD IS NEAR TO ALL
who call on him,
TO ALL WHO CALL ON HIM IN TRUTH.
PSALM 145:18

Surely your goodness and love
will follow me all the days of my life,
and I will
dwell in the house of the Lord
forever.
Psalm 23:6

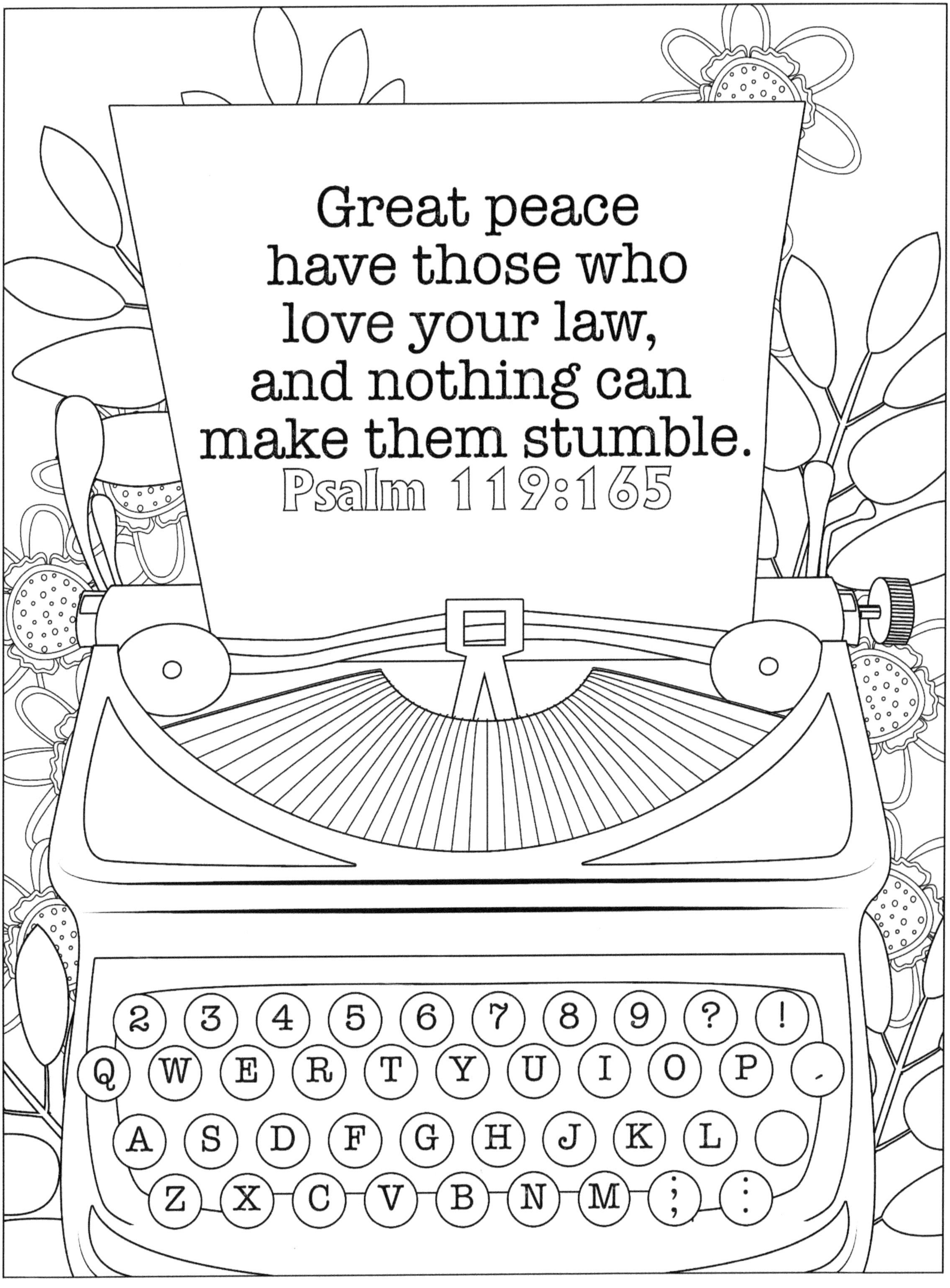
Great peace
have those who
love your law,
and nothing can
make them stumble.
Psalm 119:165
2 3 4 5 6 7 8 9 ? !
Q W E R T Y U I O P .
A S D F G H J K L
Z X C V B N M ; :

TEACH ME YOUR WAY, LORD, THAT I MAY RELY ON
YOUR FAITHFULNESS; GIVE ME AN UNDIVIDED HEART,
THAT I MAY FEAR YOUR NAME.
Psalm 86:11

He refreshes my soul.
He guides me along the right paths for his name's sake.
Psalm 23:3

My salvation and
my honor depend
on God; he is my mighty
rock, my refuge.
Psalm 62:7

The Lord is my strength
and my defense; he has
become my salvation.
Psalm 118:14

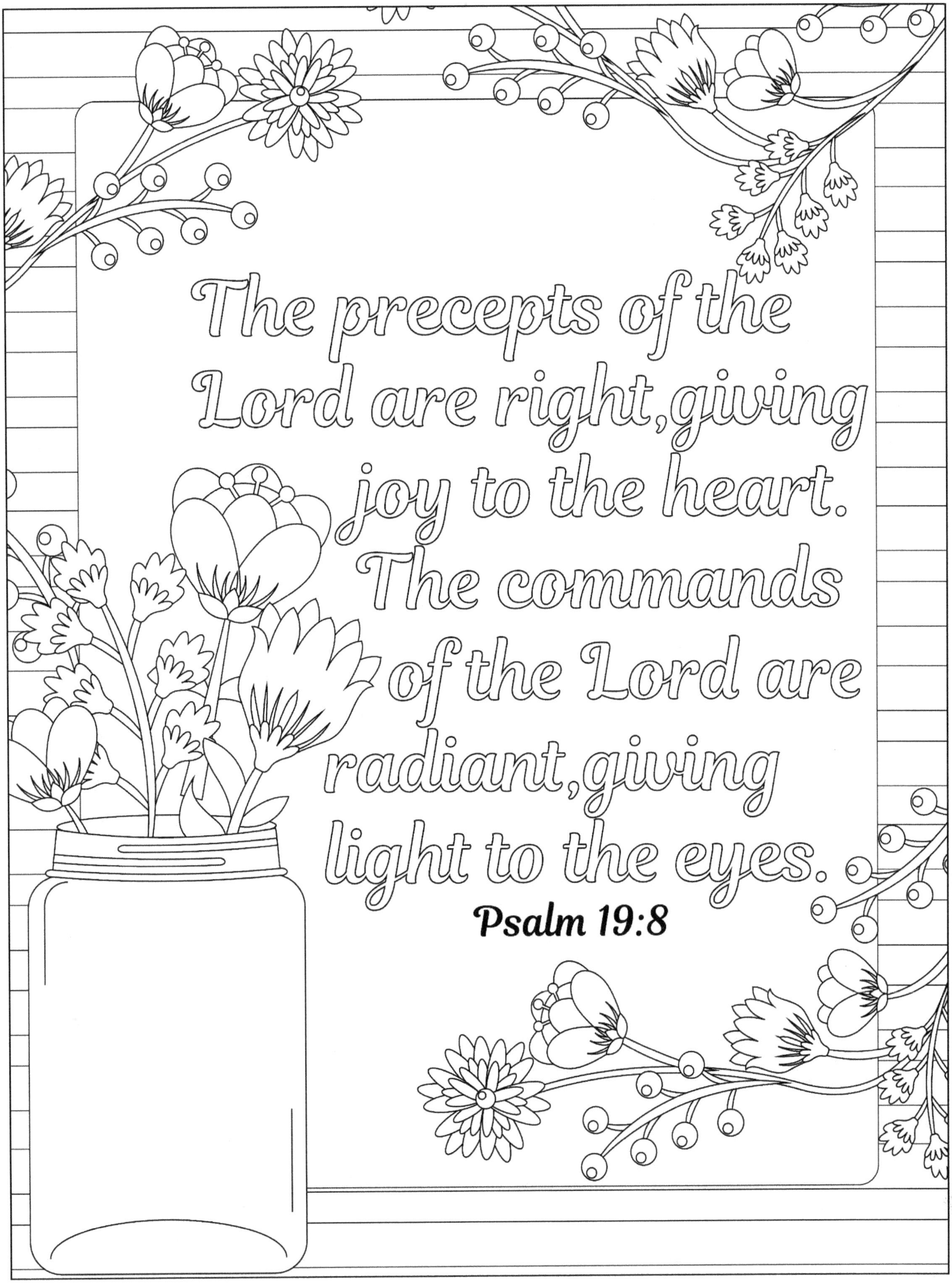
The precepts of the
Lord are right,giving
joy to the heart.
The commands
of the Lord are
radiant,giving
light to the eyes.
Psalm 19:8

CPSIA information can be obtained
at www.ICGtesting.com
Printed in the USA
LVHW062344041022
730001LV00026B/725

9 798710 547816